AND THEIR TIMES

HAN WU DI
and Ancient China

by Miriam Greenblatt

Marshall Cavendish
Benchmark
New York

ACKNOWLEDGMENT

With thanks to Dr. Morris Rossabi of the Department of
East Asian Languages and Cultures, Columbia University,
New York City, for his careful reading of the manuscript.

Marshall Cavendish Benchmark
99 White Plains Road
Tarrytown, New York 10591-9001
www.marshallcavendish.us

Text copyright © 2006 by Miriam Greenblatt
Map copyright © 2006 by Marshall Cavendish Corporation
Map by Rodica Prato

Library of Congress Cataloging-in-Publication Data
Greenblatt, Miriam.
Han Wu Di and ancient China / by Miriam Greenblatt.
p. cm. — (Rulers and their times)
Audience: Ages 11+.
Audience: Grades 7–8.
Includes bibliographical references and index.
ISBN 0-7614-1835-0
1. China—Social life and customs—221 B.C.–960 A.D.—Juvenile literature. 2. Han Wudi, Emperor of China,
156–87 B.C.—Juvenile literature. 3. China—Kings and rulers—Biography—Juvenile literature. I. Title. II. Series.
DS748.13.G74 2005   931′.04—dc22   2004000022

Printed in China
135642

Photo Research: Rose Corbett Gordon, Mystic CT
Cover: The Granger Collection, New York
Photo Credits: Page 1: Private Collection/Paul Freeman/Bridgeman Art Library; pages 2, 56, 64, 70, 73: British
Museum/Bridgeman Art Library; page 5: Erich Lessing/Art Resource, NY; pages 6–7: Bettmann/Corbis; page 9: Bibliotheque
Nationale, Paris/Archives Charmet/Bridgeman Art Library; page13: Bibliotheque Nationale, Paris/Bridgeman Art Library;
page 14: Private Collection/Archives Charmet/Bridgeman Art Library; pages 18, 32, 71: The Metropolitan Museum of Art,
Gift of The Dillon Fund, 1973 (1973.120.3) Photograph © 1994 The Metropolitan Museum of Art; page 22: The Art
Archive/Genius of China Exhibition; pages 25, 40, 67: The Art Archive/Musée Cernuschi Paris/Dagli Orti; pages 26–27, 29,
39, 43, 68: The Granger Collection, New York; pages 34, 45: Bridgeman-Giraudon/Art Resource, NY; page 49: The British
Museum; page 53: The Great Wall, China/Bridgeman Art Library; page 57: Werner Forman/Art Resource, NY; page 58:
Asian Art & Archaeology, Inc./Corbis; page 59: Royal Ontario Museum/Corbis; pages 60–61: The Art Archive; page 63 top:
Museum of Fine Arts, Houston, Texas/Gift of Carol & Robert Straus/Bridgeman Art Library; pages 63 bottom, 66, 69: Réu-
nion des Musées Nationaux/Art Resource, NY.

Permission has been granted to use extended quotations from the following copyrighted works:

"Confucius" from *Sources of Chinese Tradition,* edited by Wm. Theodore de Bary, Wing-tsit Chan and Burton Watson, 1960.
"How the World Was Made" from *Gitting: The Peach Blossom Forest and Other Chinese Legends,* by Robert Manton and
    Jo Manton, 1951.
"Li Furen" by Liu Che, Emperor Wu of Han, translated by Arthur Waley from *Classical Chinese Literature: An Anthology of
    Translations. Vol. 1: From Antiquity to the Tang Dynasty,* edited by John Minford.
"Song of Sorrow" from *The Columbia Book of Chinese Poetry: From Early Times to the Thirteenth Century,* translated and
    edited by Burton Watson, 1984.
Women in Traditional China: Ancient Times to Modern Reform, by Susan Hill Gross and Marjorie Wall Bingham, 1980.
"The Xiongnu" from *Chinese Civilization: A Sourcebook,* 2nd ed., edited by Patricia Buckley Ebrey, 1993.
"Yin and Yang in Medical Theory," from *Chinese Civilization: A Sourcebook,* 2nd ed., edited by Patricia Buckley Ebrey, 1993.

Contents

The Han's Most Famous Emperor

The civilization of China is one of the oldest in the world. It began in the valley of the Yellow River more than five thousand years ago. The earliest historical relics of city life date from about 1750 B.C.E.*

At first the Chinese people were organized into several independent states. Then in 221 B.C.E., the state of Qin (pronounced Chin) conquered the other states and established the Chinese Empire. The name *China* comes from *Qin*. Between 206 B.C.E. and 220 C.E., the Chinese Empire was ruled by a dynasty, or family, called Han. The Han dynasty was so great that many Chinese still call themselves "Sons of Han."

In this book, you will read about the Han dynasty's leading emperor, Han Wu Di. Although we know little about his personal life, we know a great deal about his numerous accomplishments. Among other things, he almost doubled the size of the Chinese Empire, reformed its government, and opened up a trade route between China and the West.

You will also read about how the ancient Chinese people

---

*Many systems of dating have been used by different cultures throughout history. This series of books uses B.C.E. (Before Common Era) and C.E. (Common Era) instead of B.C. (Before Christ) and A.D. (Anno Domini) out of respect for the diversity of the world's peoples.

This model of a horse-drawn chariot from the Han dynasty was found on an archaeological dig in China in 1969. Not only the emperor rode in style: each high-ranking official in the Han government was provided with a chariot of his own.

lived—the clothes they wore and the foods they ate, their religious beliefs and their ways of having fun. You'll learn too about the great inventions they gave to the world. Finally, you will hear the Chinese tell us about their world in their own words—through their legends, poems, and histories.

PART ONE

Han soldiers stand guard over enemy prisoners. Chinese generals spent a great deal of time studying the military tactics laid out in *The Art of War*. Written in the fifth century B.C.E., *The Art of War* is the world's oldest military handbook. It emphasizes psychological as well as physical warfare. The aim is to upset the enemy so that he will make mistakes on the battlefield.

The Martial Emperor

Son of Heaven

Han Wu Di was born as Liu Ch'e in 156 B.C.E. His father was Jing Di, fifth ruler of the Han dynasty. A few historians think Liu Ch'e was the emperor's eldest son. Most historians, however, believe he was the eleventh of Jing Di's fourteen sons. As such, he would ordinarily never have ascended the throne. But it seems that even at an early age, he showed great intelligence, vigor, and determination. Accordingly, relatives of Jing Di persuaded the emperor to name Liu Ch'e his heir when the lad was seven. Liu Ch'e was approaching his sixteenth birthday when be began his reign, in 140 B.C.E. He received the temple name of Wu Di, or "Martial Emperor," after his death.

The Chinese looked upon their emperor as the Son of Heaven. He was not a god himself, but he served as a link between the gods and the Chinese people. The Chinese believed the gods gave the emperor his right to rule, a belief known as the Mandate of Heaven. However, an emperor kept his mandate only so long as the gods approved of his behavior. If he allowed misery and war to afflict the land, he lost this mandate. Then the people could rebel and put a new emperor on the throne.

Wu Di's lifestyle was designed to distinguish him from ordinary people. He had an immense wardrobe of silk robes, with a different one for each particular occasion. He had numerous horse-drawn chariots that carried him everywhere. His living quarters were in the innermost part of the palace. Other parts were inhabited by his courtiers, his women, and the hundreds of servants who prepared his food and medicines and carried out various religious duties. Ordinary Chinese were not allowed within the palace grounds.

Wu Di sets out from his palace. This painting, done on silk, was made in the 1600s as part of a visual history of the Chinese emperors.

As the intermediary between Heaven and the Chinese people, Wu Di performed many religious ceremonies. Among the most important was welcoming the four seasons. In spring, he went out the east gate of his capital city of Changan (modern-day Xi'an) and plowed several furrows as an example to all Chinese farmers. In summer, dressed in yellow, he went out the city's south gate and offered a sacrifice to Earth. In fall, he went out the west gate to welcome the new season. And in winter, wearing blue, he exited the north gate and made sacrifices to Heaven.

Another religious ceremony was the pilgrimage to Mount Tai, in eastern China. After climbing to the top of the mountain, Wu Di presented burnt offerings, possibly of sheep or pigs, to Heaven and Earth. Then he deposited jade tablets inscribed with reports of how well he was performing his duties. Also inscribed on the tablets were prayers for the future.

In addition to seeking the blessings of Heaven on his rule, Wu Di's journeys to Mount Tai formed part of his search for immortality. He built towers in Changan that he hoped would attract the attention of the spirits. He also encouraged individuals who were trying to discover the elixir of life, a drink that would enable whoever drank it to live forever. Once, a religious group claimed to have succeeded. Wu Di immediately ordered the chief priest of the group to prepare the elixir for him. Several courtiers felt the emperor was being fooled, but he paid them no attention.

On the appointed day, the priest appeared in court and presented a cup to the emperor. Before he could take the cup, one of his courtiers grabbed it and drank the liquid inside. Furious, Wu Di demanded to know how the courtier dared to do such a thing. Didn't he realize that the penalty for such behavior was death?

"If the cup I have drunk is truly the elixir of life," the courtier reportedly replied, "Your Majesty cannot put me to death, for I shall live forever. And if it is not, I am glad to give my life to prove to Your Majesty how false and mischievous these magicians are who are deceiving you."

Wu Di spared the courtier's life. But he never gave up hope that, someday, someone would indeed discover the secret of life everlasting.

Domestic Changes

One of Wu Di's concerns was how to strengthen the national government. In the past, a great deal of power had belonged to local nobles. They drew their wealth from their large landed estates and paid little, if any, in taxes. They were more loyal to their own interests than they were to either the emperor or China.

Wu Di began by naming himself head of the government bureaucracy, or network of officials and administrators. He then appointed his own people to high-level government positions. The appointees' wealth and social background did not matter. For example, several men who began their careers as county clerks ended up as court secretaries working directly for the emperor. Naturally, such officials were extremely loyal to Wu Di.

Wu Di extended his influence to lower levels of government. The Chinese greatly respected people who did mental work, such as scholars and officials. Wu Di combined these two roles. He set up a university where people studied the writings of a philosopher named Kung Fu-tzu (551–479 B.C.E.), or Kung the Master, known to Westerners as Confucius. Confucius taught that society depended on people following a strong code of morals and respecting their leaders and elders. After a year of studying Confucian philosophy, the scholars received posts in local and provincial governments. By 132 B.C.E. China had a full-fledged civil service. University students were required to pass a standard examination based on

Passing the civil service examination was very difficult. Candidates had to memorize the 431,286 words in Confucius's writings in order to be able to answer the questions they were asked.

the Confucian classics in order to become public officials. This examination system lasted for almost two thousand years. The fact that government officials had a common educational background helped to hold the Chinese Empire together.

To support a stronger national government, Wu Di took over the coinage of money. Private minting was forbidden. He also established government monopolies on the production of iron, salt, and wine.

Wu Di was concerned about transportation. He ordered construction of a canal between Changan and the Yellow River. The area along the river contained much of China's population and

This painting by a modern Chinese artist shows Confucius, with three disciples, gazing at a river. The ancient Chinese were excellent hydraulic engineers. They built numerous canals, dykes, and irrigation systems to improve farming and transportation. Many are still in use.

produced much of the country's grain. Before the canal was built, the city and the river had been connected by a tributary of the Yellow River called the Wei. Transportation had been slow, however, because the Wei twisted and turned in all directions. Building the canal reduced the distance between Changan and the Yellow River by two-thirds. Now the capital's inhabitants could obtain food much more easily. In addition, the canal provided irrigation water for the farms along its banks.

Wu Di was also interested in flood control. He personally supervised the rebuilding of dikes along the Yellow River. The dikes had often collapsed in the past, allowing floodwaters to cover the countryside. Wu Di assigned tens of thousands of men to the task of rebuilding. He encouraged them at their labor by visiting the work sites and reading his own poems aloud.

Writing History

Wu Di's intellectual interests extended beyond setting up a university and writing poetry. He strongly encouraged the work of court historians. The most important such work was the *Shiji*, or *Records of the Historian*, written by Sima Qian (145–86 B.C.E.). It contained 130 chapters covering the history of China from the legendary Yellow Emperor down to Wu Di.

The *Shiji* was an innovative work. Instead of dealing only with dynasties, it stressed the importance of individuals, with biographies of emperors, generals, philosophers, and other leading personalities. It emphasized loyalty, patriotism, and the struggle for justice. It discussed such topics as China's economy, the calendar, music, religious rites, and astrology.

The *Shiji* also presented an overall theory of history. According to Sima Qian, the first few rulers of a dynasty are brave and virtuous. Then the rulers start to deteriorate and, after several generations, become tyrants. At this point, a new leader arises who overthrows the corrupt old dynasty and founds a dynasty of his own. Later Chinese historians followed this cyclical theory in their work.

Expanding Borders

While Wu Di was concerned mostly with domestic matters during the early years of his reign, he gradually began to pay more and more attention to foreign affairs.

Fighting the Xiongnu

China's most formidable enemy at the time was a group of Turkish-speaking tribes called the Xiongnu (who some historians believe were the ancestors of the Huns). In the north, they inhabited the grasslands that ran to the forests of Siberia. In the northwest, they dominated the land from Mongolia to the deserts of central Asia (roughly, present-day Xinjiang). Unlike the Chinese, they were not settled farmers but nomadic herders, who followed their flocks and herds from place to place in search of grass. They lived in yurts, or round tents made of felt, and dressed in the wool, leather, and fur their animals provided. The men were first-rate horseback riders and excellent fighters, being particularly skilled at archery. For years it had been their custom to swoop down on China's farms and cities and plunder them almost at will.

In the past, China had fought the Xiongnu only in defense. More often, it had bribed the raiders to stay away. Wu Di came up with a different idea. He would attack the Xiongnu and drive them so far from China that they would no longer be able to carry out raids.

An early morning scene at a nomad camp. Some nomads are playing musical instruments to welcome the new day, while others collect their horses and pack their saddlebags.

The wars against the Xiongnu began in 133 B.C.E. Wu Di's first strike against the nomads was a failure. Undaunted, the emperor regrouped his army and, four years later, struck again. This time he was successful. Over the next ten years, Wu Di's soldiers carried out seven major campaigns against the Xiongnu. The Chinese succeeded in scattering the nomads and pushing China's borders hundreds of miles to the west. After each campaign, Wu Di sent tens of thousands of Chinese colonists to settle the new territory and prevent the Xiongnu from using it again.

The Great Traveler

When Wu Di began planning war against the Xiongnu, he wanted to attack them from the west as well as the east. That meant forming an alliance with a tribe called the Yuezhi, who were old enemies of the Xiongnu. The Xiongnu had previously driven the Yuezhi from their homeland northwest of China, and the latter were now living some two thousand miles away in central Asia. In 138 B.C.E., Wu Di asked for a volunteer to carry a message to the Yuezhi. They would receive the friendship and protection of the Chinese Empire if they returned to their former homeland and helped China battle the Xiongnu.

The man who undertook the assignment was a young officer named Zhang Qian, who commanded the guards at the gates of the imperial palace. He set out on his journey with a caravan of one hundred men. Soon after leaving China, he was captured by the Xiongnu. They treated him well. He married a Xiongnu woman, with whom he had a son, and apparently rode and hunted freely with his captors. After several years, however, he managed to escape. But instead of returning to China, Zhang Qian continued westward, determined to carry out his emperor's command.

When Zhang Qian reached the land of the Yuezhi, he found that they had settled down and become well-to-do farmers. They had no desire to return to their nomadic ways near China. So Zhang Qian set out for home, along a somewhat different route. To his dismay, he was once again captured by the Xiongnu. This time, he managed to escape after only one year in captivity and, with his wife and son, reached Changan in 126 B.C.E. It was twelve years since he had left.

China and Its Neighbors around 100 B.C.E.

XIONGNU

Silk Road

FERGANA

← To Roman Empire

PARTHIA

YUEZHI

Himalaya Mountains

N

INDIA

0 100 200 300 400 500
miles

Han Chinese Empire

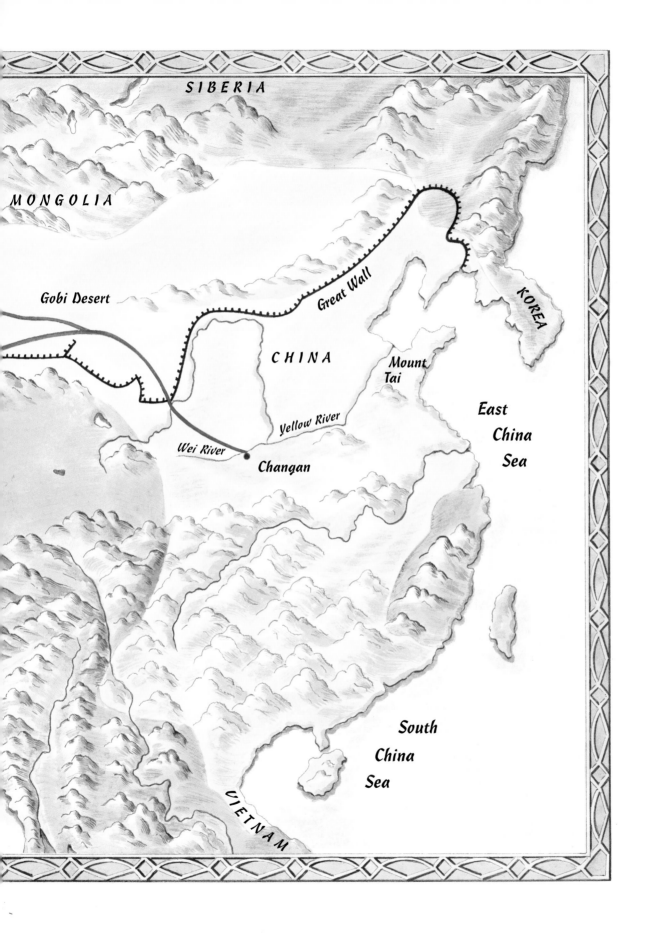

Although Zhang Qian's mission to the Yuezhi was a failure, it had unlooked-for results that brought tremendous wealth and power to China. Zhang Qian was the first Chinese to explore western Asia, and he brought back valuable information. He discovered that there was a land route between China and India. He learned about the existence of Egypt, Parthia (present-day Iran), and the Roman Empire. He brought back cuttings of alfalfa and grapes. This was the start of an exchange of plants between East and West. In succeeding years chives, cucumbers, pomegranates, sesame, and walnuts entered China, while oranges, peaches, pears, and such flowers as the azalea, camellia, chrysanthemum, peony, and rose moved out.

Horses and Silk

Perhaps the most exciting information that Zhang Qian brought back concerned the horses of Fergana (in what is now Uzbekistan). These horses were known as "celestial" or "flying" horses because of their speed. They were larger, longer-legged, stronger, and had greater stamina than the horses on which the Chinese rode. The Fergana horses also sweated blood. In the twentieth century,

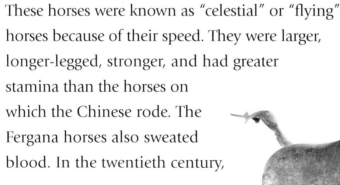

The left hind foot of this "celestial" horse rests on a swallow, probably to show that the horse could gallop faster than the swallow could fly.

people learned why. It seems that a parasite burrows under the horses' skin and creates tiny swellings that bleed when they burst.

In any event, Wu Di wanted Fergana horses for his campaigns against the Xiongnu. He also wanted control of central Asia. So for twenty-five years, he hurled army after army westward. By 102 B.C.E., China controlled not only Fergana but other central Asian kingdoms as well. The latter became vassals of China, paying tribute and sending their sons to the imperial court as a pledge of their loyalty and peaceful intentions.

The armies were quickly followed by trade. The Chinese were the only people in the world who knew how to make silk. Within a few years trains of camels loaded with the precious fabric were making their way westward. Military posts provided protection for the merchants. Cities and towns grew up around the posts, and before long the Silk Road—perhaps the most famous trade route in the world—was flourishing.

To the South and East

Another important expansion of Chinese power occurred in the south. Most of the land there was extremely fertile and at the same time comparatively empty. Wu Di's armies gradually took over the area, including what is now northern Vietnam. Hundreds of thousands of Chinese farmers and craftsmen followed the soldiers, bringing their culture with them. Most of the lands that Wu Di conquered still form part of China. The Chinese also moved eastward and established two colonies in Korea.

The Final Years

By now it was 91 B.C.E. and Wu Di had been ruling China for nearly fifty years. During that time, he had almost doubled the country's size. He had pushed the Xiongnu back for hundreds of miles. He had opened up the Silk Road. And he had established Confucian philosophy as the basis of education for government service.

Yet all was not well. The years of warfare had severely damaged the country's economy. With tens of thousands of farmers being drafted for the army each year, agriculture suffered, and food supplies ran low. At the same time, taxes kept rising. Many farmers lost their land and either fled to the mountains or were forced to become tenants on large estates. The landlords, of course, grew ever richer. And despite Confucian teachings about the importance of moral behavior, there was widespread corruption on the part of government officials.

To make matters worse, the imperial court was split between two factions. The Wei family, one of whose members was married to Wu Di, had dominated court politics for almost fifty years. Wei family members had received important public posts, as well as financial gifts from the emperor. The Li family, however, had been gradually increasing its influence. One of its members was a concubine, or secondary wife, of the emperor.

In 91 B.C.E., open warfare between the two families broke out. When the fighting was over, some ten thousand people lay dead.

As one historian wrote, "Almost the entire Wei family were exterminated and the empress committed suicide." The Li family were apparently in control. Then a Li general surrendered after an extended battle against the Xiongnu. When the news reached Changan, the tide turned against the Li family, and all its leading members were executed.

The last years of Wu Di's reign were "a time of retreat and regret." China could no longer afford to expand its borders. The government had to concentrate on supporting the economy and keeping popular unrest from turning into a national rebellion.

In the spring of 86 B.C.E., at the age of seventy, Han Wu Di fell ill. Aware that he was close to death, he named an eight-year-old son as his heir apparent. The boy's main qualification seems to have been the fact that he was not related to either the Wei family or the Li family. The emperor also appointed a triumvirate—a group of three men—to act as advisers to the boy.

Two days later, the Martial Emperor was dead. His reign of fifty-four years was one of the longest in Chinese history.

Until he was fifty-six years old, a Han soldier could always be called back into the army if an emergency arose.

PART TWO

Farmers in southern China were usually able to grow two crops of rice a year—one in early summer, the second in fall. Before the Han dynasty, people in parts of northern China considered rice a luxury. They also believed it had healing powers.

Everyday Life in Ancient China

The "Three Ways"

China's religious and philosophical beliefs were known as the "Three Ways." They were Confucianism, Daoism, and Buddhism. Each belief emphasized a different approach to life.

Confucius lived about three hundred years before the reign of Han Wu Di—at a time when China was made up of several states that were constantly warring with one another. Accordingly, Confucius preached the importance of good government and peaceable relations between people. A good ruler, Confucius said, should behave so as to set an example for his subjects. He should be both kind and just, and should use force only as a last resort. In return, people should respect and obey their ruler. The same principles applied to the family. If the family was strong, Confucius said, then the society would be stable and flourishing.

Daoism developed around the same time as Confucianism and was based on the teachings of Lao Zi, or "the Old Philosopher." Lao Zi emphasized the importance of living simply and in harmony with nature. He did not like rules and regulations. So he disapproved of the emphasis Confucius put on duty to the state and the family. The best government, according to Lao Zi, was that which governed least. Lao Zi did not like war and believed that a wise man met both good and evil with goodness.

Daoists believed in immortality. They worshipped eight "immortals" who had the power to become invisible, turn objects into

According to legend, Lao Zi (in the center of this wall painting) was seventy years old when he was born. The figure to his right is the Jade Emperor, ruler of nature.

gold, and raise the dead. Some Daoists spent considerable time trying to discover the elixir of life.

Buddhism came to China from India, probably in the first century C.E. It was founded around 500 B.C.E. by Siddhartha Gautama, who became known as the Buddha, or "Enlightened One." The Buddha taught that people's souls are reincarnated, or reborn in new bodies, as part of a continuing cycle of life and death. How you behave in one lifetime determines your soul's experience in the next lifetime. If you behave well, you may be reborn as a wise and prosperous person or as a being in heaven. If you behave badly, you may be reborn as a poor and sickly person or even a being in hell. Buddhism teaches that people can escape reincarnation and avoid the pain and suffering of life if they give up their attachment to worldly pleasures and follow the Noble Eightfold Path. Among the Path's guidelines are being open-minded, speaking the truth, saying nothing to hurt others, not committing theft or murder, meditating, and valuing shared goals such as peace rather than individual goals such as wealth. Eventually, people will reach a peaceful state called nirvana. Then the cycle of rebirth and suffering will be broken.

In addition to its ideas, Buddhism offered the Chinese people a satisfying ritual, complete with chanting, beautiful sculptures and paintings, the smell of incense, and the sound of bronze gongs. By the fourth century C.E., Buddhist monasteries dotted the country-side. Many carried such gentle names as The Voice of the Waters and The Rock of the Peaceful Mind.

Buddhism also brought to China the architectural tower known as a pagoda. Built to house sacred writings and religious relics, a pagoda has three to fifteen stories, each of which has an upward-curving tiled roof. Most pagodas were built of brick, with a facing of colored and glazed tiles. The Chinese believed that a pagoda brought good luck to the area around it and to the people living there.

Life in the City: Changan

During the Han dynasty, China's population numbered about 60 million. Of these, about 6 million lived in cities. The largest city was Changan, which contained some 250,000 inhabitants.

The Chinese believed the world was square-shaped. So they built their cities square-shaped to match the world. Straight, wide streets ran north-south and east-west through Changan, dividing it into blocks known as wards. Each ward was surrounded by a wall whose gates were locked at night to the beating of drums. Another wall surrounded the city as a whole.

Within each ward were narrow alleys jammed with houses. The main streets were lined with open-fronted shops where you could buy all sorts of items: silks; pots and pans made of brass, iron, or wood; live animals, especially pigs; and of course food, both cooked and uncooked. You could also buy food from hawkers who carried their wares around in baskets and on trays. Other people in the streets told fortunes, gave haircuts, or begged. Adding to the congestion were the horse-drawn carriages of the rich. Both horses and carriages gleamed with decorations of silver and gold.

Changan boasted two huge marketplaces where farmers brought their produce from the countryside, strollers gossiped

People and animals mingle on a crowded city street.

with one another, and public entertainers such as acrobats, dancers, and sword jugglers performed. The marketplaces had another use, too. They served as execution grounds for traitors and other criminals.

Changan contained several imperial palaces. They were built of brick, stone, or sometimes of clay and wattle that was plastered and then painted red and white. Roofs were made of pottery tiles.

Each palace contained at least one large audience hall flanked by gateways and towers. There were also a number of towers scattered throughout the city. Some had a religious purpose, such as insuring the survival of the Han dynasty; others served as astronomical observatories.

Near each palace stood gardens, shrines, and often a hunting park. Members of the court could relax in a pavilion or hunt such animals as bears, tigers, panthers, and wolves. The usual hunting technique was to set fire to the bushes in which the animals were hiding and then pursue them either on foot or in a horse-drawn chariot.

Changan's rich people lived in multistoried houses built of wood on top of a stone or concrete platform. The higher the platform, the more important was the person living there. Each house contained at least one courtyard that provided light and ventilation for the surrounding rooms. The courtyards were usually decorated with pots of flowers, a goldfish pond, and sometimes a small tree. Windows were covered with sheets of waxed paper; floors, with wool or fur rugs. Painted or embroidered silk hung on the walls. People slept on wooden beds and covered themselves with blankets stuffed with silk. They sat on cushions or low wooden couches and stored their dishes and clothing in wooden cupboards and chests.

The facades of rich people's houses were carved and painted, and many were decorated with tiles. The main doors were often guarded by a pair of stone lions. To the left of the door stood a male lion playing with a ball. To the right stood a female lion carrying a cub. The tile roofs curved up at the corners. The Chinese believed that demons could travel only in a straight line.

A miniature clay house, found in a Han Chinese tomb. This type of house was usually inhabited by craftworkers and tradespeople.

So the roofs' upturned corners served to confuse the demons and keep them away.

Poor people lived in one-story mud houses with roofs that were thatched with straw. Some houses contained only one room and were often built partly underground. Other houses contained three rooms, of which the middle one was higher than the two side rooms. There was a fireplace at one wall. Floors were covered with bamboo mats that also served as mattresses. Pillows were made of pottery or wood.

Life on the Farm

Most Chinese lived in the countryside on small, family-owned plots of land. The main crops grown in the north were millet and wheat. The main southern crop was rice.

The Han dynasty saw several technological improvements in agriculture. For example, many northern farmers began to plow their fields with iron plowshares instead of less efficient wooden ones. The iron plowshares, which were manufactured in government-run iron foundries, came in two sizes. A small pointed plowshare could be pushed by one person. A large plowshare called for a team of oxen to pull it.

The main problem for northern farmers was providing water for their crops. Rainfall was limited, and most fields were terraced, or carved out of hillsides, to prevent soil erosion. Sometimes farmers carried the water from wells and canals up to the fields in buckets. At other times, they used wooden waterwheels worked by foot pedals to raise and move the water through irrigation ditches. Most waterwheels took two people to operate.

After the grain was harvested, the farmer removed the outer shells, or husks, a process known as winnowing. Most farmers used the traditional technique of shaking the grain in a basket and tossing it into the air to let the husks blow away. During the Han dynasty, however, hand-powered machines for winnowing gradually came into use. After the grain was winnowed, it was crushed and then ground by millstones. Most millstones were worked by hand, but here and there some were turned by oxen.

Southern farmers grew rice in fields called paddies, which were separated from one another by low walls of earth. First a farmer flooded his paddy. Then he plowed it, drained it, and sowed rice seed thickly in one area. When the rice plants were about twelve inches high, the farmer would pull them up, separate them, and replant them several inches apart throughout the entire paddy. Then he would flood the paddy again. After the rice was harvested, it was piled in bundles and left to dry in the sun.

Although farmers concentrated on growing grain for food, in a few areas they were able to add to their income by keeping fish farms or maintaining bamboo groves. Some farmers grew fruit. Others cultivated vegetables and seasonings, while still others raised silkworms. Turning grapes into wine and breeding pigs for market were also common activities.

Chinese farmers made extensive use of fertilizer, which they obtained from composted plant material, such as weeds, and from animal and human waste. They mixed the fertilizer with soil before spreading it on growing crops.

A farmer's life was hard. In addition to farming his land and paying taxes, he had to serve two years in the army. He was also required to spend a certain amount of time each year on public projects, such as building roads and canals or working in the government-owned iron and salt mines. Floods, droughts, and epidemics of disease were common. If worse came to worst, he might be forced to sell his children into slavery. Small wonder that farmers often became beggars and even bandits, while peasant uprisings broke out repeatedly.

Family Traditions

What mattered most in Chinese society was not the individual but the family. The Chinese wrote their family name first, followed by their personal name. Family size varied during the four hundred years of the Han dynasty. At first a family included only parents and two or three children. Near the end of the dynasty, however, large extended families became the norm among the upper class. These usually consisted either of three generations—grandparents, parents, and children—or else of several brothers plus their wives and children.

The father was the head of the family, and children were expected to obey him without question. They were also expected to stand up straight in his presence and never do anything disrespectful such as spitting or blowing their noses.

Linked to the importance of the family was the custom of ancestor worship. The Chinese believed that when people died, they became spirits that could either help or harm the living. Accordingly, every household contained an altar where the family placed offerings of food and drink to keep their ancestral spirits happy. Rich people often built temples for this purpose. Shrines honoring the imperial ancestors stood in all the major cities. Bringing honor to your ancestors was a person's main reason for trying to succeed in the world. If you committed a crime, you shamed not only yourself, but all your ancestors as well.

Having a son was considered essential for a Chinese family. That was because only males could perform the proper rituals to honor the family's ancestors. Also, only a male could inherit the family's property. The sole exception to the rule of inheritance was a daughter's dowry, which in any event went to her new husband's family when she married. A rich man without a son would either adopt one from a blood relative or else add a concubine to his household in the hope that she would bear a son if his wife could not.

Children were given a personal name by their father three months after they were born. When they were initiated into adulthood, they received a new name that replaced their childhood name. Boys were usually considered adults at the age of twenty, girls at the age of fourteen.

If you were an upper-class male, you underwent a special capping ceremony when you became an adult. First, a plain cap was placed on your head, and the attendant priest prayed that you would obtain more money and have a happy old age. From then on, you were expected to always wear this cap in public. Next, you received two ceremonial hats. One showed that you were willing to fight in defense of the Chinese people. The other showed that you were ready to carry out the rituals of ancestor worship.

Men usually married between the ages of sixteen and thirty; women, between the ages of thirteen and sixteen. Marriages were arranged by the parents of the bride and groom through a go-between. After the marriage, the bride was considered part of her husband's family.

A woman could not obtain a divorce, but a man could divorce his wife for one of seven reasons: not bearing a child, committing adultery, disobeying her in-laws, stealing, developing an incurable disease, being jealous, or talking too much. The divorce would not go through, however, if (1) the wife had no relatives to take her in, (2) the husband had become rich during the marriage, or (3) one of the wife's in-laws had died during the past three years and she was still in mourning.

The corpses of poor Chinese were buried in a pit. Sometimes they were placed inside a wooden coffin, but usually they were simply wrapped in matting. It was customary to wash the dead person's body and hair and to clip his or her fingernails and toenails before burial.

The corpses of rich Chinese were dressed in silk before being placed inside a coffin that was either painted or lacquered. The coffin was then put in an underground vault made of brick or stone. In addition to the coffin, the tomb contained clothes, food, drink, lamps, and cooking pots, as well as pottery models of servants and animals—in short, everything a person might need beyond the grave. Scenes of happy events in the dead person's life were often painted or carved on the tomb's walls. Covering the tomb itself was a mound of earth up to ten feet high.

This bronze statue of a servant holding an oil lamp was discovered in the tomb of a member of the Han imperial family. A sliding door controls the amount of light the lamp throws off.

Food and Drink

Most Chinese ate a basic diet of grain, soybeans, vegetables, and fruit. People either ate the grain whole or else ground it into flour for noodles and dumplings. Vegetables included bamboo shoots, cabbage, celery, lotus roots, mung beans, onions, peas, radishes, and turnips. Fruit included apricots, melons, peaches, pears, persimmons, and plums. Fish was either cooked fresh with a sauce made from pickles, plums, and vinegar, or was preserved in salt for future use. Meat came

A statue of a fish merchant. Most of the fish the Chinese ate came from the country's rivers and lakes. Only a few fish were caught in the sea.

from such animals as chickens, deer, dogs, ducks, geese, and pigs, but only rich people ate it on a regular basis. Everyone drank tea, of which there were three main types: black (coppery-colored leaves), green (yellowish green leaves), and oolong (yellowish brown leaves).

Rich Chinese enjoyed giving banquets at which they served such delicacies as pigs stuffed with dates, bird's nest soup, baked owl, quails with oranges, and bears' paws. Travelers and soldiers on campaign carried dried foods with them.

The Chinese cut their food into bite-size pieces before cooking. In order to conserve fuel, they cooked their food quickly, usually in an iron frying pan called a wok. Sometimes they steamed food in a double saucepan. Herbs and spices were added to create special tastes such as sweet, sour, or hot. Popular spices included cinnamon, flower petals, garlic, ginger, leeks, mustard, scallions, sesame seeds, shallots, star anise, and tangerine peels.

Because food was cut up before cooking, people did not need knives and forks. Instead, they used wooden or ivory chopsticks to take the food out of small bowls. Poor people's bowls were made of pottery; rich people's bowls, of lacquered wood.

Upper-class Chinese had strict rules as to how to behave at mealtime. You were supposed to take only small mouthfuls and to chew them quickly without making a noise or a face. You were not supposed to swill your soup, roll grain into a ball, or pick your teeth. Also prohibited was throwing bones to the dogs.

Clothing and Adornment

Rich and poor people in ancient China dressed very differently.

Rich people wore robes of fine silk with a large sash at the waist. Sometimes the men wore tunics over long trousers. These were likewise made of silk, as were the shoes, which had thick wooden soles. Boots were made of leather. The clothes were decorated with belt and garment hooks. These were usually made of bronze inlaid with silver, gold, and semiprecious stones. In winter, rich people wrapped themselves in furs, especially squirrel, fox, leopard, and lamb.

Poor people wore clothes made of hemp, a coarse fabric woven from plant fibers. Both men and women wore a loose tunic or shirt over baggy trousers that ended just below the knees. Shoes were of woven straw. In winter, poor people wrapped themselves in quilted jackets or sheepskins.

Both men and women wore their hair long, usually tied in a topknot. You cut your hair only when a close member of your family died. Rich women's hairdos were so elaborate that they often took an hour or more each morning to prepare. The hair was twisted, combed, and piled high in the current style and was held in place with hairpins and combs of silver and gold. Sometimes the women would pin a jade ornament over their topknot.

This emperor's silk robe is typical of the elaborate clothing worn by scholars, high-ranking officials, and members of the imperial court.

Rich women used a great deal of makeup. They covered their faces with white lead or rice powder; painted their eyebrows blue, black, or green; and applied rouge, mixed with safflower and cinnabar, on their lips and cheeks. They cleaned wax from their ears with a bronze or jade scoop and plucked their eyebrows with bronze tweezers. At the beginning of the Han dynasty, fashionable eyebrows had sharply pointed tops. By the dynasty's end, curving arches were more popular.

Important Inventions

The ancient Chinese were an extraordinarily inventive people. By the time of the Han dynasty, they had invented silk, paper, the wheelbarrow, the seismograph (a device to measure earthquakes), the kite, the chest harness, and the sternpost rudder.

Silk making developed as far back as 3000 B.C.E. During the reign of Wu Di, it was one of China's leading industries and was operated by the government.

The silk-making process starts with raising silkworms, which feed on mulberry leaves. At a certain point, the silkworms spin cocoons of silk around themselves. The Chinese would unwind the silk filaments, twist them into thread, and weave the thread into a strong, beautiful, and comfortable fabric. Silk came in various densities, from heavy damask to fine gauze. Only members of the Chinese upper class were allowed to wear it. Most of the silk produced was exported westward over the Silk Road.

The earliest Chinese writing was carved on animal bones and tortoise shells. Then the Chinese began painting in black ink on strips of bamboo, which were cheaper and easier to use than bone. However, the strips were only wide enough for one column of characters. As a result, Chinese writing ran from top to bottom rather than left to right. Several strips of bamboo could be tied

Silk-making techniques in China changed little over the centuries. This scene was painted in the 1500s.

together into a bundle that served as a book. But a bamboo bundle was awkward to handle. So scholars began to write on silk, which could be rolled into a scroll. A silk scroll was flexible and easy to carry. But silk for writing rather than clothing was both scarce and expensive. So the Chinese began looking around for another material.

Historians are not certain exactly when paper was invented. Some historians attribute its discovery to Ts'ai Lun, who lived in the first century C.E. Other historians believe it was in use hundreds of years earlier. In any event, the Chinese produced paper by combining rags, tree bark, and hemp; boiling the mixture; and then straining the pulp and spreading it out to dry. Paper soon replaced other writing materials. It was cheap to make, easy to handle, and took ink well. By the ninth century C.E., the Chinese were also using paper for such products as napkins, toilet tissue, wallpaper, and paper money.

The invention of the wheelbarrow is usually credited to Chuko Liang (181–234 C.E.). Peasants used the device to take their grain, vegetables, and other farm products to market. Soldiers used it to move supplies and to carry the dead and wounded off the battlefield.

The seismograph was invented in 132 C.E. by Zhang Heng, an astronomer at the imperial court. It consisted of a large copper kettle with a mechanism inside that indicated in which direction an earthquake had occurred and how severe it was.

The Chinese invented kites about three thousand years ago. Soldiers used them to carry messages and to frighten the enemy in battle. Engineers used them to carry bamboo lines across river gorges while bridges were being built. Fishermen used them to carry bait to distant fishing holes. Children played with them for fun. Later, the Chinese flew kites to celebrate festivals and special events. The kites were made of paper, silk, or wood and often took the shape of real or mythological animals.

A throat harness allows an animal to use only about half of its pulling power. The Chinese developed a harness that went around an animal's chest. That meant people could use the full strength of an ox or a horse to pull plows and to draw carriages and carts.

The sternpost rudder enabled seamen to steer much larger vessels than before. Chinese oceangoing junks measured as much as 200 feet in length, weighed 1,500 tons, and carried several hundred crewmen. Most of the passengers—who stayed in cabins above deck—were merchants traveling to overseas markets. Since the trips were long, the merchants would bring their families with them. They also brought along buckets filled with dirt in which to grow their favorite vegetables.

Scientific Advances

The ancient Chinese not only produced many inventions. They also made notable advances in science, especially astronomy and medicine.

Astronomy

Chinese astronomers were the first in the world to prepare a star chart, which they did in about 350 B.C.E. Using only the naked eye, they selected and located some eight hundred stars, whose position they measured in degrees from the equator. The star chart was a great navigational aid to oceangoing junks.

Chinese astronomers began recording eclipses more than 3,200 years ago. These are the oldest records of eclipses found anywhere in the world. Peasants explained eclipses by myths. One myth told about a turtle that lived in the moon and periodically ate it up. Another myth told about a three-legged crow that lived in the sun and did the same thing. By the first century B.C.E., however, Chinese astronomers were explaining eclipses correctly as being caused by the movements of the earth, the moon, and the sun in relation to one another.

From 613 B.C.E. on, Chinese astronomers were recording the arrival of comets. In many cases, they also described the length and brilliance of the comet's tail, its flight path, and how long it took to flash across the sky. In 28 B.C.E. the scientists began to record sunspots, comparing their size to coins and hens' eggs.

Still another discovery made by Chinese astronomers was the appearance of novas and supernovas. These are stars that suddenly increase tremendously in brilliance and then, after a few days, fade away. The reason for the dramatic change in light is that the stars have exploded into a mass of dust. The Chinese first recorded such explosions about 3,400 years ago.

Medicine

Doctors in ancient China believed that human beings were a combination of two forces called yang and yin. If the forces were in balance, a person enjoyed good health. If the forces became unbalanced, the person fell ill. A medical text from the Han dynasty explains: "When Yang is the stronger, the body is hot . . . and people begin to pant; they . . . do not perspire. They become feverish, their mouths are dry and sore, their stomachs feel tight,

The symbol in the center of the scroll represents the forces of yang and yin. Note that each force contains something of the opposing force. The Chinese believed that not only a person's health but everything in the world had to be properly balanced between yang and yin.

and they die of constipation. . . . When Yin is the stronger, the body is cold and covered with perspiration. People . . . tremble and feel chilly. . . . Their stomachs can no longer digest food and they die."

Doctors tried to restore the balance between yang and yin by various techniques, including acupuncture, herbal medicines, and moxibustion.

Acupuncture means inserting a needle into a person's body at certain points. There were 650 such points, of which 450 are still used. Western doctors today find acupuncture useful as an anesthetic and in treating arthritis and nausea.

The most popular medicinal plant in ancient China (and still favored today) was ginseng, a root believed to have numerous beneficial qualities. The Chinese people used dozens of plants for medicinal purposes. Wolfberry was said to improve eyesight. Yam was a common remedy for fatigue and loss of appetite. Euryale seed was used to treat urinary problems. Chain-fern bark served to relieve lower back pain. Mulberry was considered a sure remedy for dizziness and inner ear problems. Headaches and the common cold were treated with bugbane rhizome.

Moxibustion involved holding a burning cone or stick made from the leaves of the mugwort plant near a patient's body. The heat from the cone would stimulate the blood and nerves in the area being treated. Western doctors today use a heating pad to do the same thing.

In addition to treating diseases, Chinese doctors emphasized preventive medicine. This included eating the right foods, exercising, and cultivating mental serenity.

Fighting the Enemy

Most Chinese men between the ages of twenty-three and fifty-six were required to spend two years in military service. The typical Han army numbered between 130,000 and 300,000 infantrymen. A small number of volunteers from the upper class, who were exempt from the draft, were cavalrymen who fought on horseback. The cavalry served mostly to guard the infantry's flanks and to carry out lightning raids. Originally the army also included charioteers. But war chariots, although impressive to look at, were cumbersome and difficult to maneuver, especially over rough terrain. So after a while they were no longer used in battle.

An infantryman's armor was made of lacquered leather plates tied together by leather thongs. Crossed straps at the back held the armor over the soldier's chest and groin. A cavalryman wore a short vest made of hundreds of small iron plates. An officer's armor consisted of small iron plates over a leather foundation. He also wore a cape with tassels dangling from his shoulders.

The deadliest weapon used by the Han army was the crossbow, which the Chinese invented sometime before 450 B.C.E. A crossbow is easier to shoot than a longbow, and its arrows can travel much farther, up to 650 feet. Other weapons included iron or bronze swords, axes, daggers, knives, and especially the halberd.

This was a seven-foot-long bamboo shaft with a curved blade mounted at one end. A soldier swinging a halberd could stay out of reach of an enemy's sword during hand-to-hand combat.

Like the Chinese government, Han troops were well organized. Records were kept on every soldier, including his name, age, birthplace, and status. Officers received annual performance ratings. Weapons and supplies were inventoried on a regular basis. Financial accounts were always expected to be up to date. Nevertheless, generals had considerable leeway in managing their troops, and the degree of discipline varied from one army to another.

In addition to being well armed and well organized, the Han military employed a number of defensive strategies. An extensive spy system helped ferret out information about enemy movements. Barbed iron balls placed on the ground outside a city wall helped keep off attacking soldiers.

Perhaps the best defensive strategy the Chinese developed was the Great Wall, which ran along the country's northern frontier. The Great Wall was originally a series of walls that had been built by different Chinese states. In 214 B.C.E. China's first emperor connected the individual walls into a single wall almost 1,500 miles long. The project took seven years and required hundreds of thousands of workers. Wu Di had the wall repaired and also extended it 300 miles farther west into the Gobi Desert.

The weather along the desert frontier ranged from tropical heat in summer to thirty degrees below zero in winter. The workers mixed gravel with water and piled the mixture on top of willow twigs for strength. Then they stamped on the mixture for about an hour to make it compact. Slowly the wall went up, layer by layer.

In most places, it measured about twenty-five feet high and twenty feet thick.

Square watchtowers of plastered and whitewashed bricks stood along the wall at intervals of 180 to 200 yards. This was close

The Great Wall is the longest structure ever built. It has sometimes been called the "Longest Graveyard in the World." That is because so many workers died while building it and were buried alongside.

enough to send signals from one tower to the next. Daytime signals were sent by smoke or by red and blue flags. Nighttime signals were sent by fire. Piles of brushwood or timber were always stacked nearby. The north side of the wall was lined with sandbanks. These were kept smoothly raked so that any movement or intrusion would be clearly visible.

The soldiers stationed along the Great Wall had many duties. In addition to watching for enemy movements, they were charged with protecting the merchant caravans that moved along the Silk Road. They supervised the markets that sprang up at the Great Wall's gates. They served as border police and customs agents, checking on travelers in both directions to make certain that they were not criminals, deserters, or smugglers. Some soldiers were assigned to grow grain and other crops for food. Other soldiers worked on local irrigation projects.

Cultivating the Arts

Chinese artists devoted much of their time to the "three perfections." These were calligraphy, or writing; poetry; and painting.

The Chinese did not have an alphabet. Instead, they wrote with characters called pictograms. Each pictogram represented an object or an idea. Sometimes several pictograms were combined to form a new meaning. For example, a rising sun behind a tree meant "east." China's first dictionary, which was presented to the emperor in 121 C.E., contained more than nine thousand pictograms. No wonder the Chinese respected those who knew how to read and write!

A calligrapher used brushes made out of wolf or goat hair and a black ink made by mixing pine soot with lampblack. After glue was added, the ink was shaped into a cake or a stick. The calligrapher wrote on silk, wood, paper, or bamboo. The brushstrokes varied in width and had to be drawn "gracefully and in the right order."

Both Wu Di and the founder of the Han dynasty wrote poetry, and upper-class Chinese followed their example. Many poems dealt with nature or with the end of a human relationship. Other poems described the luxurious life at the imperial court. The poems often imitated the style of poems in the *Shijing*, or *Book of Poetry*, a collection of old hymns and folk songs.

Painting became popular some time after the Han dynasty.

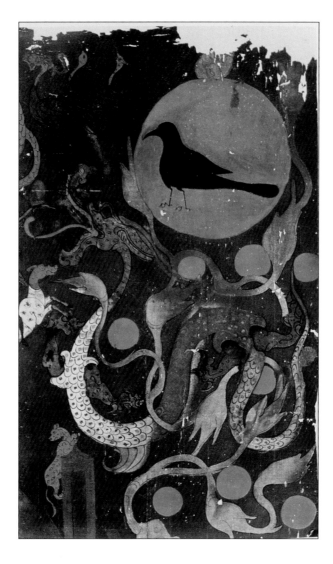

This painting was done on a silk scroll. The background was originally a warm red that has turned brown over the years.

Painters used the same tools and techniques as calligraphers. However, painters usually had a larger collection of brushes. There were brushes with long hairs for applying a wash to the background of a painting. There were small brushes for detail work. Many paintings showed landscapes, especially of mountains and water. Others pictured farming scenes. Painters used colored inks as well as black. The colors included red, brown, silver, indigo, yellow, and oyster-white.

Han craftsmen turned out beautiful bowls, boxes, and similar objects of lacquerwork. Lacquer is a juice that comes from the lac tree. When applied to fabric or wood and allowed to dry, it creates a smooth, hard, waterproof surface that can be either painted or engraved. The most common colors used in lacquerwork were red and black, but by the end of the Han dynasty, craftsmen were also using green, yellow, blue, silver, and gold. Much of the lacquerware was produced in government-operated workshops. Different workers performed different parts of the process, such as applying the base coat, painting the design, and polishing the surface.

The figures on this lacquer basket portray children listening obediently to their parents. Respect for one's elders was an important part of Han Chinese society.

Having Fun

People in Han China celebrated several national holidays. The festival of the New Year, which marked the beginning of spring, lasted fifteen days. Its high point was a family feast at which everyone exchanged gifts. It was also the custom to visit all one's relatives, no matter how far away they lived. Not welcoming a visitor meant that you would have bad luck for the coming year. At the end of the New Year Festival came the Lantern Festival, during which people waved lanterns made of glass, horn, paper, or silk. Another national festival was the Qinming, which honored ancestors. People would visit ancestral graves, sweep them clean, and leave offerings of food.

Dancers always performed to music, either sung or played on an instrument. Some dances were presented at court banquets. Other dances were part of religious rituals. These lively figures and the ones opposite were created during the Han dynasty.

Poor people in China often spent their free time gambling with dice or betting on cockfights and dog or horse races. Rich people played various board games that resembled backgammon, lotto, and chess. They hunted such animals as wild boars, deer, and rabbits, and enjoyed archery and a kind of football.

A couple of men play a game with gambling sticks. The sticks were probably shaken out of a pot onto the table. The ancient Chinese used similar kinds of sticks to tell fortunes.

Rich people also maintained private orchestras. The typical orchestra contained five instruments. The *sheng* was a mouth organ made of bamboo pipes. Several *sheng* were usually played at the same time. The *qin* was a kind of lute, with seven strings that were plucked by hand. The *qin* gave off a gentle, rather sad sound. Other popular instruments included the drum, the flute, and chimes.

The Han Chinese had a great respect for music. Official banquets at the imperial court were always accompanied by an orchestra. So were religious rituals. Confucius believed that certain kinds of music led to inner harmony, while other kinds led to violent behavior. Music, in his view, should be morally uplifting.

PART THREE

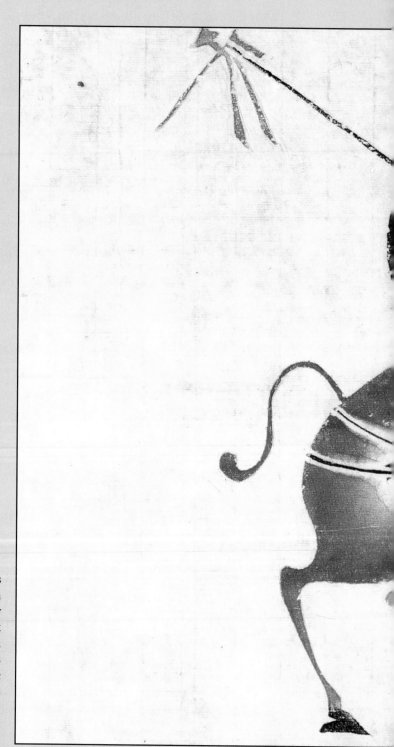

The "celestial" horses Wu Di obtained from Fergana were extremely valuable. It is said that each horse was worth three hundred pounds of gold. Rich Chinese had models of horses buried with them to indicate their wealth and social position.

The Ancient Chinese
in Their Own Words

Like most civilizations, China has a creation story.

In the morning of time there was no sand, no sea, no cold blue waves, no tides to wash beneath the shining moon. There was no earth, no vast sky, no green or living thing—only a huge emptiness. Then an eggshell cracked and out stepped Pan Ku, who made the world.

He was a shaggy dwarf, with two horns on his head. Later he wore a bearskin in winter and a green leaf cloak in summer; but from the first he had a hammer and chisel and with these he set to work. He hammered and chiseled for eighteen thousand years, making the heavens and the earth. Each day Pan Ku grew six feet taller than the day before, yet even he needed help with his great task. So four fabulous beasts came to help him.

First a great flying lizard, the dragon, rose into the sky; there it beat its glittering scaly tail against the clouds and made rain. Next came the phoenix bird with dazzling plumage. . . . Next came the unicorn, with one horn in the centre of its forehead. . . . Last came the tortoise, full of wisdom. To help Pan Ku, it held up the four corners of the earth on its four feet and solid shell.

These four and Pan Ku made the universe, but it was still empty. Now came the time to clothe it with life. So Pan Ku dissolved, becoming the thing that he had made. His breath became the wind and clouds, his voice the thunder, his blood the rivers, his flesh the soil, his bones the rocks and precious stones.

As for the fleas that lived in his shaggy hide, they hopped out and became our ancestors, the first men and women.

This design of a dragon carrying a soldier decorated a brick used in building a Han tomb.

Then the dragon made more rain, and wherever it fell on the hills and valleys of earth, ferny green grew in shoots curled like the phoenix tail. . . . Colors were born; red in the morning sky, black in the cloud, green in the pine, and white in the shining snow. Yet the world still lived in darkness, for there was no day or night; the sun and the moon were still asleep at the bottom of the China Sea. So Pan Ku's ghost wrote the Chinese character for sun *in his left hand and that for* moon *in his right. Then he went down to the white stony shore and, holding out each hand in turn, repeated a charm seven times. When they heard this, the sun and moon woke up and flew to their places in the sky. . . .*

So with earth, sun, moon, men and women, day and night, the world was made; nor have any of these things changed since.

Unlike the mythical dragon, phoenix, and unicorn, the giant panda is a real animal native to China. A member of the bear family, it has white fur with black markings. Han emperors considered the giant panda a symbol of courage and strength and kept several in the imperial gardens in Changan.

The Chinese have a legend about how the giant panda, which they called *beishung*, got its markings. A shepherdess named Dolma would take her flock of sheep to a meadow in the mountains to graze. One day, a white *beishung* cub came out of the forest. Dolma invited it to eat something and play with her sheep. A few days later, the cub was suddenly attacked by a snow leopard that jumped down from a tree. Dolma grabbed a branch and began to hit the leopard. Releasing the cub, the leopard attacked Dolma instead. Within a few minutes, she was dead. When the day came for her funeral, the people of her village filled the air with their lamentations. The *beishung*, grateful that Dolma had saved the cub from the leopard, joined in the funeral procession. The legend continues:

> As the bamboo grasses rustled in damp winds, the mourners smeared themselves with ashes. The Beishung wiped their tear-filled eyes with sooty paws and hugged themselves as they wept. They covered their ears against the loud lamentations and, wherever the animals touched their snowy bodies with ash, the black soot stained forever the thick white fur. . . . This is exactly why to this day, the giant panda, the "bamboo-eater," wears the black marks of mourning in memory of the brave shepherdess, Dolma.

—From *The Legend of the Panda* © 1998 by Linda Granfield, published by Tundra Books

Another animal beloved by the ancient Chinese is the cat, as can be seen from the following story.

There are as many tales of clever cats as there are cats' tails in China. Only listen and you will hear.

Once upon a time there lived a happy farmer. Within his bamboo fence and mud wall, he was king. His terraced hills grew [soybeans, grain, and vegetables]. . . . Even his waste land grew thickets of bamboo-shoots, delicious boiled in the pot in spring. His children drove out the ducks and geese to the pond, and led them home at twilight, safe from the prowling fox. At break of day he shouldered his hoe and trudged out; until yellow evening-cloud he hoed his crops. When he woke at night and heard rain patter down on the thatch, he was happy to think of his thirsty seedlings. . . .

Then, suddenly, all this happiness was at an end. For a huge evil rat, larger than a boar, gnawed its way into his barns and devoured all the year's crops which he had stored there. What use to plough and sow, water and weed, simply to make a rat grow fatter? No trap was big enough to catch it, no poison strong enough to kill it, and as for the yellow chow dog, it ran away howling at the sight of that fierce-whiskered snout. . . .

Then a neighbour came to the kitchen door, carrying under his arm a small, homely grey cat.

"My unworthy self and humble cat venture to save your honourable home," said the visitor politely. Even in their trouble, the farmer and his wife could not keep from laughing.

"Why, that poor little creature!" cried the farmer's wife. "The rat will finish her with one snap of its jaws!"

"I boldly venture to disagree," said the neighbour.

He set the cat on the table, left the outer door ajar, and nudged them to hide behind the stove. Instantly the rat rushed in snarling and leaped on to the table to devour the cat. The cat jumped to the floor, landing soundlessly on grey velvet paws. The rat jumped after her. Instantly, with no apparent effort, the cat was on the table again, four paws neatly collected. . . . The rat charged after her, its mean little red eyes glaring angrily. The cat, with studied indifference, leaped to the floor. This pantomime went on for ten full minutes, while the neighbour, the farmer and his wife watched from their hiding-place. The rat's sides grew dark with sweat, and froth from its ugly jaws spattered table and floor; the three in hiding could hear it gasp at each jump. The cat, by contrast, had not a whisker out of place. The rat dragged itself slowly and heavily to its feet at each fall, until at last it lay panting, unable to move. Instantly the grey cat pounced on it, breaking its neck with one neat nip of her dainty muzzle. Then she jumped back on the table and began composedly washing face and paws.

The farmer and his wife broke into loud cries of thanks and admiration. "Your wonderful cat has saved our home," they said. The neighbour made polite gestures to show that all this was nothing; it would have been exceedingly ill-mannered to praise his own property. Yet he could not deny the cat's cleverness. "Faithful cat—farmer's friend," he said.

When the author of this book was a little girl, she used to play a game called "Confucius says." Below are some of the things Confucius actually said in conversations with his disciples. The sayings were collected in a book titled *Analects*.

Education

Confucius said: "By nature men are pretty much alike; it is learning and practice that set them apart."

Confucius said: "Those who are born wise are the highest type of people; those who become wise through learning come next; those who learn by overcoming dullness come after that. Those who are dull but still won't learn are the lowest type of people."

Humanity

Confucius said: "Do not do to others what you would not want others to do to you. Then there will be no dissatisfaction either in the state or at home."

The Gentleman

Confucius said: "The gentleman is always calm and at ease; the inferior man is always worried and full of distress."

This painted clay jar in the shape of an owl was used for storing wine.

Confucius began teaching when he was twenty-two years old. After twenty-five years, he left teaching and spent thirteen years visiting different Chinese states and offering their rulers advice on how to govern. He then returned to his home state and resumed teaching. He died at the age of seventy-three.

Confucius said: "The gentleman understands what is right; the inferior man understands what is profitable."

Confucius said: "The gentleman makes demands on himself; the inferior man makes demands on others."

Government by Personal Virtue

Confucius said: "The essentials [for ruling a country] are sufficient food, sufficient troops, and the confidence of the people."
Tzu Kung [a disciple] said: "Suppose you were forced to give up

one of these three, which would you let go first?" Confucius said: "The troops." Tzu Kung asked again: "If you were forced to give up one of the two remaining, which would you let go?"

Confucius said: "Food. For from of old, death has been the lot of all men, but a people without faith cannot survive."

Another Chinese who offered advice was Ban Zhao, a historian at the Han imperial court. In addition to a history of the Han dynasty and numerous poems, she wrote a book entitled *Lessons for Women*.

> *Let a woman retire late to bed, but rise early to duties; let her not dread tasks by day or by night. Let her not refuse to perform domestic duties whether easy or difficult.*
>
> *To choose her words with care; to avoid vulgar language; to speak at appropriate times; and not to weary others (with much conversation), may be called the characteristics of womanly words.*
>
> *Whenever the mother-in-law says, 'Do not do that,' and if what she says is right, unquestionably the daughter-in-law obeys. Whenever the mother-in-law says, 'Do that,' even if what she says is wrong, still the daughter-in-law submits unfailing to the command.*

Chinese poems often dealt with a loss of one kind or another. The first poem below is believed to have been written by Han Wu Di, after the death of his concubine, Li Furen. The second poem was written by a Chinese princess who was sent to marry a nomad chief with whom the Han emperor wanted to establish friendly relations.

Li Furen

The sound of her silk skirt has stopped.
On the marble pavement dust grows.
Her empty room is cold and still.
Fallen leaves are piled against the doors.
Longing for that lovely lady
How can I bring my aching heart to rest?

Song of Sorrow

My family has married me
  in this far corner of the world,
sent me to a strange land,
  to the king of the Wu-sun.
A yurt is my chamber,
  felt my walls,
flesh my only food,
  kumiss to drink.
My thoughts are all of my homeland,
  my heart aches within.
Oh to be the yellow crane
  winging home again!

A Xiongnu chieftain sits next to his Chinese wife in their camp. A woman in such a situation had great trouble adjusting to nomadic customs, food, and housing.

In the *Shiji*, Sima Qian described the peoples who lived outside China's borders. The following excerpt deals with the Xiongnu.

The Xiongnu . . . [raise mostly] horses, oxen, and sheep, but also keep unusual animals like camels, asses, mules, and wild horses. . . . They have no written language, so make oral agreements. Little boys are able to ride sheep and shoot birds and mice with bows and arrows. When they are somewhat older they shoot foxes and rabbits for food. Thus all the men can shoot and serve as cavalry.

It is the custom of the Xiongnu to support themselves in ordinary times by following their flocks and hunting, but in times of hardship they take up arms to raid. This would appear to be their nature. Bows and arrows are the weapons they use for distant targets; swords and spears the ones they use at close range. When it is to their advantage, they advance; when not they retreat, as they see no shame in retreat. . . . The strongest eat the best food; the old eat the leftovers. They honor the young and strong and despise the old and weak. A man . . . whose brother has died marries his brother's wife. They only have personal names, no family names or polite names, and observe no name taboos. . . .

Each year in the first month all the chiefs, large and small, assemble at the Shanyu's (ruler's) court to make sacrifices. In the fifth month there is a great assembly at Long Fort, where they make sacrifices to their ancestors, to heaven and earth, and to gods and spirits. In the fall, when the horses are fat, there is a major assembly at Dai Forest, where the people and animals are assessed and counted.

According to their laws, anyone who draws his sword a foot is killed. Those who commit robbery have their property confiscated. For minor offenses people are flogged and for major ones executed. No one stays in jail awaiting sentence more than ten days, and there are never more than a few prisoners in the whole country.

Every morning the Shanyu leaves the camp and bows to the sun as it rises; in the evening he bows to the moon. At a feast, the honored seat is the one to the left or the one facing north. They favor the days wu and ji in the ten-day week. In seeing off the dead, they use inner and outer coffins, gold and silver ornaments, and clothes and furs, but do not construct mounds or plant trees over the grave or put on mourning garments. Sometimes up to several hundred or several thousand favored subordinates or concubines follow their master in death.

In making decisions, the Xiongnu take note of the stars and moon; when the moon is full, they attack; when it wanes they retreat. In battles, those who decapitate an enemy are given a cup of wine and whatever booty they have seized. Captives are made into slaves. Consequently, when they fight, they all compete for profit. They are good at setting up decoys to deceive the enemy. When they see the enemy, eager for booty, they sweep down like a flock of birds. If surrounded or defeated, they break like tiles or scatter like mist. Anyone who is able to bring back the body of someone who died in battle gets all of the dead man's property.

Glossary

civil service: All government employees except soldiers.

dowry: The money or property that a bride brings to a marriage.

dynasty: A series of rulers from the same family.

elixir: A potion.

filament: A hairlike strand of material.

indigo: Dark blue.

infantryman: A soldier who fights on foot.

junk: A flat-bottomed sailing ship with a high rear deck.

kumiss: Fermented mare's milk.

monopoly: Exclusive control over a commercial activity.

parasite: An insect or other organism that feeds and is sheltered on an animal but contributes nothing to its host.

pavilion: A light, roofed structure, often with open sides.

philosopher: A person who thinks deeply about life and the world; a lover of wisdom.

Shiji: A book on the history of China from the legendary Yellow Emperor down to Wu Di.

Shijing: A collection of old poems, hymns, and folk songs.

tribute: The forced payment of money or property.

tunic: A long, loose-fitting garment, either sleeved or sleeveless, often worn belted at the waist.

vassal: Someone controlled by or dependent on someone else.

wattle: A framework of interwoven twigs, slender branches, or reeds.

yurt: A round, domed, portable tent used by central Asian nomads.

For Further Reading

Allison, Amy. *Life in Ancient China.* San Diego: Lucent Books, 2001.

Carpenter, Frances. *Tales of a Chinese Grandmother.* Clarendon, VT: Charles E. Tuttle, 1972.

Cotterell, Arthur. *Ancient China.* New York: Alfred A. Knopf, 1994.

Fisher, Leonard Everett. *The Great Wall of China.* New York: Macmillan, 1986.

McNeese, Tim. *The Great Wall of China.* San Diego: Lucent Books, 1997.

Nicholson, Robert, and Claire Watts. *Ancient China.* New York: Chelsea House, 1994.

Teague, Ken. *Growing Up in Ancient China.* Mahwah, NJ: Troll Associates, 1994.

ONLINE INFORMATION*

http://www.historyforkids.org/learn/china/
"Ancient China"

http://www.historylink101.com/china_history.htm
"Ancient China"

http://members.aol.com/Donnclass/Chinalife.html
"Daily Life in Ancient China"

http://www.silk-road.com/artl/wuti.shtml
"Han Emperor Wu-ti's Interest in Central Asia and Chang Chien's Expeditions"

http://www.cs.uiowa.edu/~yhe/poetry/han_poems.html
"Selected Poems from Han Dynasty to Northern and Southern Dynasties"

*All Internet sites were available and accurate when this book was sent to press.

Bibliography

Cotterell, Arthur. *Ancient China.* New York: Alfred A. Knopf, 1994.

Ebrey, Patricia Buckley, ed. *Chinese Civilization: A Sourcebook.* 2nd ed. New York: The Free Press, 1993.

Granfield, Linda. *The Legend of the Panda.* Toronto: Tundra Books, 1998.

Gross, Susan Hill, and Marjorie Wall Bingham. *Women in Traditional China.* Saint Louis Park, MN: Glenhurst Publications, 1980.

Harrison, John A. *The Chinese Empire.* New York: Harcourt Brace Jovanovich, 1972.

Loewe, Michael. *Everyday Life in Early Imperial China.* New York: Dorset Press, 1988.

Manton, Jo. *The Flying Horses.* New York: Holt, Rinehart and Winston, 1977.

Martell, Hazel Mary. *The Ancient Chinese.* New York: Macmillan, 1993.

Minford, John, and Joseph S. M. Lau, eds. *Classical Chinese Literature.* New York: Columbia University Press, 2000.

Paludan, Ann. *Chronicle of the Chinese Emperors.* London: Thames and Hudson, 1998.

Pirazzoli-t'Serstevens, Michele. *The Han Dynasty.* New York: Rizzoli, 1982.

Ross, Frank, Jr. *Oracle Bones, Stars, and Wheelbarrows.* Boston: Houghton Mifflin, 1982.

Schafter, Edward H. *Ancient China.* New York: Time-Life Books, 1967.

Seeger, Elizabeth. *The Pageant of Chinese History.* New York: David McKay Company, 1962.

Seybolt, Peter J. *Through Chinese Eyes.* New York: CITE Books, 1988.

Twitchett, Denis, and Michael Loewe, eds. *The Cambridge History of China.* Vol. 1. Cambridge: Cambridge University Press, 1986.

Watson, Burton, ed. *The Columbia Book of Chinese Poetry.* New York: Columbia University Press, 1984.

Notes

Part One

Page 11 "If the cup I have drunk": Seeger, *The Pageant of Chinese History*, p. 140.

Page 25 "Almost the entire Wei family": Paludan, *Chronicle of the Chinese Emperors*, p. 39.

Page 25 "a time of retreat and regret": *The New Encyclopaedia Britannica*, Vol. 12, p. 781.

Part Two

Page 49 "When Yang is the stronger": Ebrey, *Chinese Civilization: A Sourcebook*, p. 78.

Page 55 "gracefully and in the right order": Cotterell, *Ancient China*, p. 31.

Part Three

Page 62 "In the morning of time": Manton, *The Flying Horses*, pp. 10–11.

Page 65 "There are as many tales": Manton, *The Flying Horses*, pp. 154–156.

Page 67 *Education:* Confucius said": Seybolt, *Through Chinese Eyes*, pp. 107–109.

Page 69 "Let a woman retire": Gross and Bingham, *Women in Traditional China*, p. 36.

Page 70 "The sound of her silk skirt": Minford and Lau, *Classical Chinese Literature*, p. 416.

Page 70 "My family has married me": Watson, *The Columbia Book of Chinese Poetry*, p. 75.

Page 72 "The Xiongnu . . . [raise mostly] horses": Ebrey, *Chinese Civilization: A Sourcebook*, pp. 55–56.

Index

Page numbers for illustrations are in **boldface**.

pictograms, 55
plants, medicinal, 50
poetry, Chinese, 55, 70

religious and philosophical
    beliefs, Chinese
    Buddhism, 29, 29–30
    Confucianism, 28
        Daoism, 28–29
    religious ceremonies,
        10–11
rice paddies, 35

scientific advances, 48–50,
    49
seismograph, invention of,
    44, 46
Shiji (Sima Qian), 16, 55,
    72–73
silk-making process, 44, **45**
Silk Road, 23, 25, 44, 54

sternpost rudder, invention
    of, 44, 47

trade, foreign, 22, 23
transportation, 14–15
Ts'ai Lun, 46

vassals, 23

Wei family, 24–25
wheelbarrow, invention of
    the, 44, 46
women, Chinese, **71**
    clothing and adornment,
        42–43
    family traditions, 37–39
    Lessons for Women
        (Ban Zhao), 69
writings, Chinese, 16, 44,
    46, 55
    animal stories, 64–66

Confucian sayings,
    67–69, **68**
creation story, 62–63,
    63
Lessons for Women
    (Ban Zhao), 69
poetry, 55, 70

Xiongnu, **71**
    wars against the, 17–19,
        18, 23, 24, 25
    writings about the,
        72–73

yang and yin, forces of,
    49–50, **49**
Yellow River, 4, 14–15
Yuezhi tribe, 19, 22

Zhang Heng, 46
Zhang Qian, 19, 22

About the Author

"As far back as I can remember, I have been interested in people who came before me—how they lived, what they thought, and what their leaders were like. The desire to know and understand is probably one reason why my favorite reading is mysteries, especially those set in ancient times and different cultures."

In addition to reading mystery novels, Miriam Greenblatt acts in community theater and is an avid adventure traveler. She has rafted rivers in Sumatra and Papua New Guinea, ridden a camel in India and an elephant in Thailand, and explored cities from Tokyo to Timbuktu. She is the author of several history textbooks, three presidential biographies for teenagers, and twelve titles in the Rulers and Their Times series. She lives in a northern suburb of Chicago with her two cats, Batu Khan and Barnum.